Rise Above and Just... Live

Rebecca Little

Presentation by *BookLeaf Publishing*

Web: www.bookleafpub.com

E-mail: info@bookleafpub.com

ISBN: 978-93-95755-54-2

First edition 2022

She Hides It Well

She hides it well
The daily pain her body provides
She hides it well
The internal battle she fights
In her very own place in hell

She hides it well
The desire to be loved, mixed with
the underlying fear it will all end up the same
She hides it well
Behind the walls she's built
Where hardly anyone remains

A strong independent woman
Who fights her battles alone
Not because she wants too, no
but because she has to
Everybody leaves at some point
Everybody breaks her somehow
But with the masks in place and smile upon her
face
She certainly hides it well

Sometimes

I may smile, but that doesn't mean I'm okay
I may laugh, but that doesn't mean that I don't
struggle to make it through the day
I may tell you I'm fine but sometimes
Sometimes, that's my biggest lie

Chronic Illness

I walk, I'm in pain
I write, I'm in pain
I eat, I'm in pain
But I hide it well
Through a smile
Positivity and optimism
Even though I'm secretly
Making my way through the pits of hell

A Simple Task

An internal battle she fights
A daily pain her body provides
Today, will she be able to walk?
How about a task as simple
As holding a spoon?
It would be nice
If she were able to tell
Which body parts are
Going to put her through hell

Won't

I could back down and cry
But I won't
I could let it get the better of me
But I won't
I could just give up…
But I won't

Phoenix

Like the phoenix
I will rise through the ashes
What was once weak
Now extremely strong
You see the flames
Shine brighter and I burn
The higher I rise
Remember my power
As you take in this
Glorious Sight

Adventuretime

Take my hand and let's go
On a crazy adventure
Into the unknown
I'll be your Bonnie
If you'll be my Clyde
Let's go on this crazy ride
Together side by side

Count The Reasons

Let me count the reasons why these walls
prevent you from getting inside…

For years they have protected my fragile heart,
keeping the unworthy at bay
It has become such a habit that I've even told the
worthy they cannot stay
I'm not crazy, but I can get paranoid
Forever overthinking, constantly believing the
worst is yet to come
When I open up and give someone my trust
It tends to go wrong
They lie, they cheat, they leave
Many other things can occur
But this I do not wish to confer
What hurts the most is
I have a lot of love to give
And a heart worn on my sleeve
Family, lovers, friends
Well… they all end up leaving
in the end

And this is… why I make it so hard to just let
anyone in
So, remember that the next time you start asking
me all these personal kind of questions.

Selfish

If I reached out to you tonight to say I need a
friend
would you be there?
If I told you I was still struggling
would you care?

If I asked you to lend me your ear
so, I could I have someone
to listen to my pain, would you do it?

The answer is no, no you won't
And that my dear is the most painful thing of
all…

Goodbye Friend

Awake at 5am
These tears in my eyes are enough
To confirm this tough decision
I need to put you in the rear view vision
For my own state of mind
I need to break these bonds
I love you with all my heart
But you've left me with no choice
For both my mental state and yours
I'm walking away
I'm sorry but I can no longer be
Your punching bag… I mean rock

Heal Me

I'm not sure where this is going
But I'm happy with the path it's taking
Day by day everything gets a little brighter
I don't know if that's me or if it's you
Who is slowly healing me inside

Get to know you

This smile is becoming real
The more I get to know you
The happiness is creeping back
The more I get to know you
I'm still a little guarded
But I'm glad to have met you
And I'm thankful you are here
As the more I get to know you
The more I see that someone can
And does, see the beauty inside of me

Lockdown Number???

It's days like these where I feel numb
The constant unknown is crippling
Too much uncertainty is overwhelming
Not sure how more of this I can take
The walls are closing in there's nothing I can do
Confined to this place, until strangers tell me it's
safe
To venture out into the world again
Almost 200 days and counting
I think we're all over it now

Let her Out

A tear shed silently in the night
Sleep evading her yet again
The frustration grows deeper
The anger explodes from within
She needs to be let out
She needs to be set free
Can no longer be caged
Can no longer be isolated

Reality

Look at the mirror and what do you see?
Reality or make believe?
Are there walls surrounding your heart?
Is there a mask hiding the true person you are?
So many of us are afraid to be true to ourselves
Afraid to reveal to others who we are
It's a great tragedy when you've got a lot of love
to give but can't express it in the best way you
know how
That's what trauma does to you. It generates a
fear that is hard to let go of
But when you finally do… watch just how
brightly your souls shines, watch as true blissful
happiness envelopes you

Hold Me

Take my hand and hold it tight
Whisper to me and let me know that everything
will be alright
Tell me that these dark days will subside and
that happiness will return once again
Let me know that you will be by my side and
that I no longer have to hide
That you have my back through all this pain and
even more so once I'm whole again…

HeartBreak

I want to be in your arms again
How can I bring you back?
Tell me how things can mend
You were more than a partner
You were my best friend
I just want to pick up the phone and hear your
voice on the other end
I want you to tell me that everything is going to
be ok
I wish that our love would somehow find a way
A way to mend two hearts back to one

You

I wonder if you consider yourself a coward
Do you think about the things you said to me?
Do you cringe as you look back at the
destruction you've caused?
Do you lie awake at night with a mind full of
regret?
I hope you do…
I hope one day you will open your eyes and
realise the problem was in front of you all along
It was You

She's The Girl

She's the girl who hides behind the walls
The ones she put up to keep others out
To keep them from getting too close
To keep them from breaking her like others have
done before
She's the girl with a heart of gold
Who's love is strong & true
But you need to know the right way to get
through
To have her trust, her love and desire
Is something so very few ever get to admire.
She's the girl who's walls are so high
To keep the pain and trauma at bay
Enter if you dare, & have the strength to push
through
To show her that not everyone leaves her …in
the end.

Not Temporary

I would like it if I were the one
Instead of the one of many
It would be nice to be the reason
You smile and to be the first thing
You think of each morning
And the last thought as you fall asleep at night
But these are just distant dreams...
However...
I'm not a temporary solution
Someone to just warm your bed
I'm worth more than just a second glance
I'm not a second option when no other is
available
I deserve a chance, I deserve respect
Instead of hearing see you later, next

The Storm

I am the storm
Can you withstand it?
I am its strength, I am its power
I laugh in the face of adversity
If you're with me, then embrace it
If not, then get the hell out of my way

www.ingramcontent.com/pod-product-compliance
Lightning Source LLC
Chambersburg PA
CBHW061326140726
47998CB00007B/2564